CAN I TRUST
the BIBLE?

THE CRUCIAL QUESTIONS SERIES
BY R.C. SPROUL

CRUCIAL
QUESTIONS
№. | 2

CAN I TRUST
the BIBLE?

R.C. SPROUL

Ⅰ̶R Reformation Trust   A DIVISION OF LIGONIER MINISTRIES, ORLANDO, FL

Can I Trust the Bible?

© 2017 by R.C. Sproul

Published by Reformation Trust Publishing
A division of Ligonier Ministries
421 Ligonier Court, Sanford, FL 32771
Ligonier.org   ReformationTrust.com

Printed in North Mankato, MN
Corporate Graphics
November 2017
2017 edition

ISBN 978-1-56769-849-7 (Paperback)
ISBN 978-1-56769-912-8 (ePub)
ISBN 978-1-56769-913-5 (Kindle)

Cover design: Gearbox Studios
Interior design and typeset: Katherine Lloyd, The DESK

Scripture quotations are from the ESV® Bible (The Holy Bible, English Standard Version®), copyright © 2001 by Crossway, a publishing ministry of Good News Publishers. Used by permission. All rights reserved.

Material in this book has previously been published in *Everyone's a Theologian* (2014). Some material in this book has previously been published as *Explaining Inerrancy: A Commentary* (1980) and as *Explaining Inerrancy* (1996).

Library of Congress Cataloging in Publication Control Number: 2017023437

Contents

Chapter One

SPECIAL REVELATION

In the 1970s, Harold Lindsell published a book titled *The Battle for the Bible*. In that book, Lindsell addressed what had become a huge matter of controversy—the truthfulness and reliability of the Scriptures. In the face of myriad arguments against the inspiration, infallibility, and inerrancy of the Bible, Lindsell took a stand and declared that the Bible remains trustworthy.

It was this same desire to stand against the persistent

questioning of the Bible's integrity that brought together more than 250 evangelical leaders in Chicago in October 1978. That summit meeting, convened by the International Council on Biblical Inerrancy, sought to draw a line in the sand, affirming the historic Protestant position on the Scriptures. The result was the Chicago Statement on Biblical Inerrancy.

The issue of the Bible's reliability is crucial. It is via the Scriptures that the church historically has claimed to understand matters of faith and life, from God's creation of all things out of nothing to the significance of the life, death, resurrection, and ascension of Jesus Christ to the ultimate consummation of all things toward which history is moving. If the Bible is unreliable in what it teaches about these things, the church is left to speculate and has nothing of value to speak to the world.

In the years since the summit meeting, the battle for the Bible has not abated. It is more crucial than ever that believers understand what the Bible is and why they can trust it wholeheartedly. Christians still need to be equipped with the understanding of why they can and should trust the Bible.

THE NATURE OF REVELATION

Christianity at its heart is a revealed religion, and there is a content to that revelation. The issue of the nature of divine revelation focuses on a question that's been disputed for ages, not least in the twentieth and twenty-first centuries. Theologians have offered other explanations for what revelation is, how we have received it, and how it can be understood and interpreted. This is the disagreement that is at the heart of the battle for the Bible: whether God can and does reveal Himself in a way that people can understand. Historically, the church has affirmed that God reveals Himself, and that He does so in two distinct ways: through general revelation and special revelation.

General revelation is just that: general. It is available to people everywhere. The Bible speaks of God as revealing Himself through nature and conscience (Ps. 19:1; Rom. 2:15). This is general revelation. It tells everyone in the world some of who God is: that He exists, that He is good, that He is powerful (Rom. 1:19–20).

Special revelation, on the other hand, is not available to everyone. It that sense, it is not general information, but its content is more specific. Special revelation discloses

God's plan of redemption. It tells us of the incarnation, the cross, and the resurrection—things that cannot be learned through a study of the natural realm. It is found primarily (though not exclusively) in sacred Scripture. The Bible bears witness to how God has revealed Himself in a special way:

> Long ago, at many times and in many ways, God spoke to our fathers by the prophets, but in these last days he has spoken to us by his Son, whom he appointed the heir of all things, through whom also he created the world. He is the radiance of the glory of God and the exact imprint of his nature, and he upholds the universe by the word of his power. After making purification for sins, he sat down at the right hand of the Majesty on high. (Heb. 1:1–3)

We receive distinct information from God Himself, and that astonishing fact lies at the root of a Christian understanding of knowledge. Epistemology (a subdivision of philosophy) is the science of knowing. It analyzes the ways in which human beings acquire knowledge. Great debates rage over whether humans learn primarily through the mind—the rational approach to knowledge—or through the five senses of sight, sound, taste, touch, and smell—the empirical approach. Even within Christian circles, the debate goes on as to whether reason or the senses are primary.

As Christians, however, we should all agree that Christianity is based ultimately on knowledge that comes to us from God Himself. Holding to that conviction is vitally important for our determination of truth, because knowledge that comes from God is far superior to anything we can deduce from an analysis of our situation, from introspection, or from observation of the world around us.

GOD SPEAKS

A crucial concept in understanding the revelation we have from God is that it is *received*. The word *received* has historical significance. Church councils used the Latin word *recipimus* (we receive) in reference to the canon; they were saying "we receive" various books to be included in Scripture. By using the word *receive*, the church made clear that it was not declaring certain books to be authoritative by its own authority; rather, they recognized the voice of God in Scripture and displayed their willingness to submit to His Word. Ultimately, they—and we—believe the Bible because it comes from God Himself.

Since the close of the canon in the first century, the Word of God alone is the means by which God speaks to the church. But previously, He spoke to His people in various ways. In Old Testament times, He spoke to people directly on occasion. There were also occasions when He revealed Himself through dreams or particular signs, as He did for Gideon. There were times when God revealed Himself through the casting of lots, through the use of the Urim and Thummim by the priests, and through theophanies. The word *theophany* comes from the Greek words *theos*, which means "God," and *phaneros*, which means "manifestation," so a theophany was simply a visible manifestation of the invisible God.

Perhaps the best-known Old Testament theophany is the burning bush that Moses encountered in the Midianite wilderness. When Moses saw a bush on fire but not consumed by the flames, he approached the bush, and God spoke audibly to Moses from the bush, saying, "I AM WHO I AM" (Ex. 3:14). The bush was a visible manifestation of the invisible God. The pillar of cloud and the pillar of fire that led the people of Israel through their wanderings in the wilderness after the exodus were also visible manifestations of the invisible God.

PROPHETS AND APOSTLES

The primary way that God communicated with the people of Israel was through the prophets, whom we call "agents of revelation." The prophets were human beings just like us. They used human language, but because they received information from God, their words functioned as vessels or conduits of divine revelation. That is why they began their prophecies by saying, "Thus says the Lord." The words of the prophets were set down in writing and became the inscripturated Word of God. Thus, the Old Testament was produced by people like us, who, unlike us, were designated by God to be His spokesmen to His people.

Of course, not everyone in ancient Israel who claimed to be a prophet was in fact a prophet; indeed, Israel's biggest struggle was not with hostile nations but with false prophets in the camp or within the gates of the city. False prophets were known for teaching what people wanted to hear rather than true revelation from God. Throughout his ministry, Jeremiah was plagued by false prophets. When Jeremiah attempted to warn the people of the impending judgment of God, the false prophets opposed Jeremiah's prophecy and did everything they could to stifle his message.

There were ways to distinguish between a true prophet and a false prophet. The Israelites were to apply three tests to determine who was a true vehicle of divine revelation. The first test was a divine call, which is why the prophets were zealous to show that they had been called directly by God and commissioned for the task. In the Old Testament, we see several of the prophets, including Amos, Isaiah, Jeremiah, and Ezekiel, recount for their audience the circumstances by which they were specifically called and anointed to prophesy.

The second test of a true prophet in the Old Testament was the presence of miracles. Not all the prophets in the Old Testament performed miracles, but their ministry was authenticated at the outset by an outburst of miracles that began with Moses and continued in the days of Elijah, and the other prophets followed in that line. Distinguishing a true miracle from a false one was a critical matter, because there were imitation miracles, such as those performed by the magicians in the court of Pharaoh. Their so-called miracles were only deceptive tricks.

The third test of a true prophet was fulfillment; in other words, did the things that the prophets announced come to pass? False prophets attempted to predict what was going to happen, but when their predictions failed to come true, their messages were proven to be false.

In the New Testament, the counterpart to the prophet was the Apostle. The chief mark of an Apostle was that he had received a direct call by Christ. The term *apostle* refers to one who is sent or commissioned with the authority of the one doing the sending. Jesus said to His Apostles, "Whoever receives you receives me, and whoever receives me receives him who sent me" (Matt. 10:40). One of the most important Apostles in the New Testament, Paul, was not one of the original Twelve. Paul presumably did not know Jesus during Jesus' earthly ministry, and he was not an eyewitness of the resurrection as the rest of them were. Paul seemed to lack the credentials necessary to be an Apostle, which is why the New Testament recounts, both through Paul's own testimony and through the testimony of Luke, the circumstances of Paul's call on the road to

Damascus. Additionally, the other Apostles confirmed the authenticity of Paul's Apostleship.

The prophets and the Apostles together form the foundation of the church (Eph. 2:20). Through both the prophets of the Old Testament and the Apostles of the New Testament, we have been given a written record of special revelation. It has come to us by the agents of Christ, His authorized agents of revelation. Jesus left no manuscript bearing His signature; He was the author of no book. Everything we know about Him is contained in the New Testament record that has come to us through the work of His Apostles. They are His emissaries, who were given His authority to speak on His behalf.

THE INCARNATE WORD

The author of Hebrews points out another dimension of special revelation, the supreme revelation, which is the incarnate Word. We have the written Word, which gives us special revelation, but we also have the Word of God incarnate, the One about whom the written Word speaks. The One who embodies the very Word of God is Jesus Himself, as the author of Hebrews declares, saying, "Long ago, at many times and in many ways, God spoke to our fathers by the prophets, but in these last days he has spoken to us by his Son, whom he appointed the heir of all things, through whom also he created the world" (Heb. 1:1–2).

When the disciples were gathered with Jesus in the upper room, Philip said to Him, "Lord, show us the Father, and it is enough for us." Jesus responded: "Have I been with you so long, and you still do not know me, Philip? . . . Do you not believe that I am in the Father and the Father is in me?" (John 14:8–10). The chief of all Apostles, the One whom God chose as His ultimate vehicle of self-disclosure, is Christ Himself. In Christ we meet the fullness of the revelation of the Father, and it is only through Scripture that we meet Christ.

Chapter Two

THE INSPIRATION AND AUTHORITY OF SCRIPTURE

The material cause of the sixteenth-century Reformation was the doctrine of justification by faith alone, but lurking behind the scenes was another important issue—authority.

When Martin Luther engaged in debate with the leaders of the Roman Catholic Church over the doctrine of justification, he was maneuvered into a position in which he had to confess publicly that his views did not agree with previous statements made by the church and with certain statements that had been issued by former popes. That provoked a crisis for Luther; questioning the authority of the church or of the pope was unacceptable in Luther's day. Luther held his ground, however, and finally, at the Diet of Worms in 1521, he said:

> Unless I am convinced by the testimony of the Scriptures or by clear reason (for I do not trust either in the pope or in councils alone, since it is well known that they have often erred and contradicted themselves), I am bound by the Scriptures I have quoted and my conscience is captive to the Word of God. I cannot and I will not recant anything, since it is neither safe nor right to go against conscience. I cannot do otherwise, here I stand, may God help me, Amen.[*]

Out of that conflict came the Reformation slogan *sola Scriptura*, which means "Scripture alone." Luther and the

---

[*] *Luther's Works*, vol. 32, ed. George W. Forell (Philadelphia: Fortress, 1958), 113.

other Reformers said that only one authority ultimately has the absolute right to bind our consciences. Luther did not demean the lesser authority of the church or the importance of historic church councils such as Nicea and Chalcedon. His point was that even church councils do not have the same level of authority that the Bible has. This focused attention on the nature of and basis for biblical authority.

AUTHORSHIP AND AUTHORITY

Fundamental to the Reformers' view of the primacy and authority of Scripture was the Bible's authorship. Notice the closeness between these two words, *authority* and *authorship*. Both contain the word *author*. The Reformers said that although the Bible appeared one book at a time and was written by human beings, the ultimate author of the Bible was not Paul, Luke, Jeremiah, or Moses, but God Himself. God exercised His authority through the writings of human authors who served as His spokesmen to the world.

How was it possible for human authors to be invested with the authority of God? The prophets, as we observed in the last chapter, claimed that their messages came from

God, and that is why two Latin phrases have historically been used to refer to the nature of sacred Scripture. One phrase is *verbum Dei*, which means "the Word of God," and the other is *vox Dei*, which means "the voice of God." The Reformers believed that although God did not personally write down the words that appear on the pages of the Bible, they are no less His words than if they had been delivered to us directly from heaven.

In his second letter to Timothy, Paul writes, "All Scripture is breathed out by God" (2 Tim. 3:16). The Greek word that is translated here as "Scripture," *graphē*, simply means "writings." For the Jewish people, however, *graphē* had specific reference to the Old Testament. Additionally, the phrase "It is written" was a technical term that they understood to have specific reference to the biblical writings. This text in 2 Timothy is very significant, because the term "Scripture" here has specific reference to the Old Testament and, by extension, incorporates the writings of the Apostles in the New Testament, as the Apostles were conscious of their own authority to deliver the New Testament Word of God communicated to them by the Holy Spirit. (For example, the Apostle Peter includes Paul's writings with the rest of the Scripture; see 2 Peter 3:16. Paul is conscious of His own authority to issue binding revelation; see 1 Cor. 7:10–16.) Paul makes an astonishing claim when he says that all of these writings, all of the *graphē*, are given by divine inspiration.

BREATHED OUT

The word translated "breathed out" in the English Standard Version is translated as "given by inspiration" in the King James Version and other translations. Given the long history of the doctrine of inspiration, we must make a distinction between the meaning of 2 Timothy 3:16 and the way that the term *inspiration* has been understood throughout the history of the church.

The theologian B.B. Warfield once pointed out that the real meaning of 2 Timothy 3:16 has to do not so much with the way in which God communicated His information (through human writers) as with the source of that information. Literally, Paul writes here that all Scripture is *theopneustos*, that is, "God-breathed," which has to do with what God breathes out rather than into what God breathes. The force behind Paul's words is that all of Scripture is breathed out from God. To breathe out is *expiration*, whereas to breathe in is *inspiration*, so technically we ought to translate this phrase as saying that all Scripture is given by "expiration of God" rather than by "inspiration." The point is that when Paul insists that all Scripture has been breathed out by God, he is saying that its ultimate origin is God. God is the source of these writings.

When we speak of inspiration as a concept, we are talking about the work of the Holy Spirit, who came upon people at various times and anointed them by His power, so that they were inspired to write the true Word of God. The Holy Spirit's work in this regard is nowhere defined in Scripture, but the Bible is clear that Scripture is not of human initiation. In sum, the doctrine of inspiration concerns the way in which God superintended the writing of sacred Scripture.

Some have charged orthodox Christians with teaching a mechanical view of inspiration—sometimes called "the dictation theory"—which is the idea that the authors of Scripture merely took dictation from God, just as a secretary writes down, word for word, a letter as it is verbally dictated. The church has historically distanced herself from this simplistic view of inspiration, although there have been times when some in the church seemed to imply that this view was true; at the Council of Trent in the sixteenth century, for example, the Roman Catholic Church used the word *dictante*, meaning "dictating," with respect to the Spirit's work in the giving of the ancient texts. John Calvin said that, in a certain sense, the prophets and the Apostles served as *amanuenses* (secretaries) for God. Insofar as they were agents to communicate God's words, they were *amanuenses*, but that does not explain the mode of inspiration.

Whatever the process of inspiration may have been, it did not override the authors' personalities as they wrote. The writers of Scripture were chosen and prepared by God for their sacred task, and an analysis of Scripture makes clear that their distinctive personalities and writing styles come through. Luke's style, for example, is obviously different from that of Matthew. The literary structures found in the writing of Daniel differ greatly from those found in the writing of James. Men of Hebrew origin tended to write in Hebraic styles, and those of the Greek cultural background tended to write in a Greek style. However, God made it possible for His truth to be communicated in an inspired way while making use of the backgrounds, personalities, and literary styles of these various writers. What was overcome or overridden by inspiration was not human personalities, styles, or literary methods, but human tendencies to distortion, falsehood, and error.

Evangelical Christians avoid the notion that the biblical writers were passive instruments like pens in the hand of God, yet at the same time they affirm that the net result of the process of inspiration was the same. Calvin, for example, says that we should read the Bible *as if* we have heard God audibly speaking its message. That is, it carries the same weight of authority as if God Himself were giving utterance to the words.* This does not mean that Calvin believed or taught that God did in fact utter the words audibly. We do not know the process by which inspired Scripture was given. But because of inspiration, however God brought it about, every word of Scripture carries the weight of God's authority.

EVERY LAST WORD

Additionally, the church has historically believed that the inspiration of the Bible was verbal; in other words, inspiration

---

* *Institutes of the Christian Religion* 1.7.1.

extends not simply to a broad outline of the information communicated by the earthly authors but to the very words of Scripture themselves. That is one of the reasons the church has been zealous to reconstruct as carefully as possible the original manuscripts of the Bible and has given such care to studying the meanings of ancient Hebrew and Greek terms. Every word carries divine authority.

When Jesus talked with Satan in the wilderness during His temptation, they debated citations from Scripture. Jesus regularly made a case against the devil or the Pharisees by the turn of a single word. He also said that not a jot or a tittle of the law will pass away until all is fulfilled (Matt. 5:18). He meant that there is not a superfluous word in the law of God or a word that is open to negotiation. Every word carries the weight of the binding authority of its ultimate author.

In our day, with the avalanche of criticism against the Bible, there have been attempts to get out from under the concept of inspiration. The German scholar Rudolf Bultmann (1884–1976) rejected the idea of the divine origin of Scripture wholesale. Neoorthodox theologians are concerned to restore the preaching of the Bible to the church and to give a higher view of the Bible than that which was left from nineteenth-century liberalism, but they also reject verbal inspiration and propositional revelation. Their approach sought to promote a "dynamic" view of the Bible that sees the authority of Scripture functioning in a dynamic relationship of Word and hearing of the Word. Several theologians have denied that the Bible, in and of itself, is objective revelation. They maintain that revelation does not occur until there is an inward, subjective human response to that Word. Scholars such as Emil Brunner (1889–1966), for example, have insisted that the Bible is not itself revelation, but is merely a witness to the revelation that is found in Christ. Karl Barth (1886–1968) said that God reveals Himself through events, not propositions. It has become fashionable in certain quarters to maintain that special revelation is embodied in Christ alone, and that to consider the Bible as objective revelation would be to detract from the uniqueness of the person of Christ, the Word made flesh.

However, the Bible is not merely a narrative record of events in which we are told what happened and then left to ourselves to interpret their meaning. Rather, the Bible gives us both the record of what happened and the authoritative, Apostolic, and prophetic interpretation of the meaning of those events. Jesus' death on the cross, for example, was both recorded for us and explained in the Gospels and Epistles. People viewed Jesus' death in different ways. For many of His followers, it caused tragic disillusionment; for Pontius Pilate and for Caiaphas, it was a matter of political expediency. The Apostle Paul, when he expounds on the meaning of the cross, frames it as a cosmic act of redemption, as an atonement offered to satisfy the justice of God, a truth not immediately apparent from simply viewing the event.

Neoorthodox theologians also say that the Bible is not revelation but a *Zeugnis*, or "witness," to revelation, which reduces the level of the Bible's authority significantly. They claim that while Scripture has some historical significance and bears witness to the truth, it is not necessarily itself the revelation. Conversely, orthodox Christianity claims that Scripture not only bears witness to the truth but is the truth. It is the actual embodiment of divine revelation. It does not simply point beyond itself; it gives us nothing less than the veritable Word of God.

Chapter Three

INFALLIBILITY
AND INERRANCY

Any discussion of the nature of sacred Scripture that includes the issue of inspiration has to tackle the issues of infallibility and inerrancy. Throughout church history, the traditional view has been that the Bible is infallible and inerrant. However, with the rise of so-called higher criticism, particularly in the nineteenth and twentieth centuries, not only has the inspiration of Scripture come under widespread attack, but the concepts of infallibility and inerrancy in particular have been sharply criticized.

Some critics say that the doctrine of inerrancy was the creation of Protestants in the seventeenth century, which is sometimes called "the age of Protestant scholasticism," corresponding to the era of secular philosophy called "the age of reason." These critics claim that inerrancy as a rational construct was foreign to the biblical writers and even to the magisterial Reformers of the sixteenth century. However, the Reformers did declare the Scriptures to be without error, as did the church fathers, including Tertullian, Irenaeus, and particularly Augustine. Even more important is the Bible's own claim to divine origin. It is significant to the church that the Bible claims to have come about through divine inspiration.

DEFINING THE TERMS

The church historically has seen that the Bible alone, of all the written literature in history, is uniquely infallible. The word *infallible* may be defined as "that which cannot fail"; it means something is incapable of making a mistake. From a linguistic standpoint, the term *infallible* is higher than the term *inerrant*. Though the words have often been used virtually as synonyms in the English language, there remains a historic technical distinction between the two. The distinction is that of the potential and the actual, the hypothetical and the real. Infallibility has to do with the question of ability or potential; that which is infallible is said to be unable to make mistakes or to err. By contrast, that which is inerrant is that which, in fact, does not err. As an illustration: a student can take a test made up of twenty questions and get twenty correct answers, giving him an inerrant test. However, the student's inerrancy in this restricted arena does not make him infallible, as mistakes on subsequent tests would verify.

Much of the controversy surrounding the issue of inspiration involves a certain amount of confusion about the terms *inerrancy* and *infallibility*, specifically, the extent to which they apply. To illustrate, note the difference in the following two statements:

A. The Bible is the only infallible rule of faith and practice.

B. The Bible is infallible only when it speaks of faith and practice.

The two statements sound similar, but they are radically different. In the first statement, the term only sets Scripture apart as the one infallible source with authoritative capacity. In other words, Scripture is the rule of our faith, which has to do with all that we believe, and it is the rule of our practice, which has to do with all that we do.

These words change their orientation in the second statement. Here the word *only* restricts a portion of the Bible itself, saying that it is infallible only when it speaks of faith and practice. This is a view called "limited inerrancy," and this way of viewing Scripture has become popular in our day. The terms *faith* and *practice* capture the whole of the Christian life, but in this second statement, "faith and practice" are reduced to a portion of the teaching of Scripture, leaving out what the Bible says about history, science, and cultural matters. In other words, the Bible is authoritative only when it speaks of religious faith; its teachings on anything else are considered fallible.

It has been fashionable in certain quarters to maintain that the Bible is not normal history, but redemptive history—with the accent on the word *redemptive*. Theories are then established that limit inspiration to themes of redemption, allowing the historical dimension to be errant.

However, the fact that the Bible is not written like other forms of history does not negate the historical dimension with which it is intimately involved. Though the Bible is indeed *redemptive* history, it is also redemptive *history*; this means that the acts of salvation wrought by God actually occurred in the space-time world.

With respect to matters of science, the further denial that scientific hypotheses about earth history may be used to overturn Scripture's teaching again rejects the idea that the Bible speaks authoritatively merely in areas of spiritual value or concerning redemptive themes. The Bible has something to say about the origin of the earth, about the advent of man, and about matters that have scientific import, such as the question of the flood. It is important to note that this is not to imply that scientific hypotheses or research are useless to the student of the Bible or that science contributes nothing to an understanding of biblical material. We are merely saying that the teaching of Scripture cannot be overturned by teachings from external sources.

HUMANITY AND ERROR

It is one thing for God to confer infallibility to the writings and quite another to confer omniscience to the writers.

Omniscience and infallibility must be carefully distinguished. Although they are conjoined in God, it is different for man. Omniscience refers to the scope of one's knowledge while infallibility refers to the reliability of his pronouncements. One who knows better can make a false statement if it is his intention to deceive. Conversely, a person with limited knowledge can make infallible statements if they can be guaranteed to be completely reliable. Thus, we say that though the biblical writings are inspired, this does not imply that the writers knew everything there was to be known or that they were infallible in themselves. The knowledge they communicated is not comprehensive, but it is true and trustworthy as far as it goes.

Opponents of biblical inerrancy such as Karl Barth have argued that such a position, by introducing the divine characteristic of infallibility, cancels out the true humanity of the biblical writers. For Barth, it is fundamental to our humanity that we are liable to err, and therefore the Bible, as the product of human authors, must be subject to error. If the classic statement is *errare est humanum*, "to err is human," we reply that though this is true, it does not follow that men always err or that error is necessary for humanity. If such were the case, it would be necessary for us to assert that Adam, before he fell, had to err or he was not human, or that Christ, being truly human, had to distort the truth. This is clearly not the case. Even apart from inspiration, it is not necessary for a human being to err in order to be human. So if it is possible for an uninspired person to speak the truth without error, how much more will it be the case for one who is under the influence of inspiration?

Finitude implies a necessary limitation of knowledge but not necessarily a distortion of knowledge. The trustworthy character of the biblical text should not be denied on the ground of man's finitude.

THE AUTHORITY OF CHRIST

In the final analysis, the question of the authority of the Bible rests on the authority of Christ. During the 1970s, Ligonier Ministries sponsored a conference on the topic of the authority of Scripture.[*] Scholars from around the world came together to discuss the question of inerrancy,

---

[*] See *God's Inerrant Word: An International Symposium on the Trustworthiness of Scripture*, ed. John Warwick Montgomery (Calgary, Alberta: Canadian Institute for Law, Theology, and Public Policy, 1974).

and with no collusion, every scholar there considered the issue from a christological standpoint: What was Jesus' view of Scripture? The desire of these scholars was to hold a view of the Bible that reflected the view of Scripture taught by Jesus Himself.

The only way we know of Jesus' view of the Bible is by reading the Bible, which is a fact that leads to a circular argument: Jesus taught inerrancy in the Bible, yet we know what Jesus said only by virtue of the Bible. However, there is widespread agreement even among the critics that the least-disputed portions of Scripture with regard to historical authenticity are those that contain Jesus' statements about Scripture. There is no serious dispute among theologians about Jesus' view of the Bible. Scholars and theologians of all backgrounds, liberals and conservatives alike, agree that the historical Jesus of Nazareth believed and taught the high, exalted view of Scripture that was common to first-century Judaism, namely, that the Bible is nothing less than the inspired Word of God. Jesus' view of Scripture is revealed in the Gospels: "Until heaven and earth pass away, not an iota, not a dot, will pass from the Law until all is accomplished" (Matt. 5:18); "Scripture cannot be broken" (John 10:35); and "Your word is truth"

(John 17:17). Additionally, Jesus frequently rested His case on the Old Testament, saying simply, "It is written," to settle a theological dispute.

There are few, if any, scholars who challenge the view that Jesus of Nazareth taught what the church for two thousand years has been teaching. However, many of those same scholars turn around and say that Jesus was wrong in His view of Scripture. One must wonder at the arrogance of such a statement from Christian theologians. They make this claim by reasoning that Jesus was influenced by the prevailing view of Scripture held by the Jewish community of His age, which, in His human nature, He did not know was erroneous. They are quick to point out to their detractors that there were things the human Jesus, despite His divine nature, did not know. When pressed about the day and the hour of His return, for example, Jesus told His disciples that no one knows it except for the Father (Matt. 24:36), and in so saying, Jesus expressed a limit to His own knowledge. This, the critics claim, excuses Jesus for giving us a false view of Scripture.

In response, orthodox scholars say that while Jesus' human nature did not have the attribute of omniscience, it was not necessary for Him to be omniscient in order to be our Redeemer. The divine nature did have omniscience, but the human nature did not. However, the deeper issue here is the sinlessness of Christ. It would have been sinful for One claiming to teach nothing except what He received from God to teach an error. The Scriptures have an ethic about teaching, that not many ought to become teachers because they will be judged more strictly (James 3:1). I have a moral responsibility as a teacher not to lie to my students. If my students ask me a question to which I do not know the answer, I am obliged to tell them that I do not know. If my thinking is tentative on the matter, I must let them know that I am unsure of the answer. Such caution is necessary because a teacher has power to influence the thinking of those studying at his feet.

No teacher in history has had greater influence and authority than Jesus of Nazareth. If He told people that Moses wrote of Him, that Abraham rejoiced to see His day, that the Word cannot be broken, and that the Scripture is true, but He was wrong, He is culpable for that; He was responsible to put a limit on His own certainty where that limit actually fell.

If Jesus was wrong in His teaching about a matter as crucial as the authority of the Bible, I cannot imagine anyone taking Him seriously about anything else He taught. Jesus said, "If I have told you earthly things and you do not believe, how can you believe if I tell you heavenly things?" (John 3:12), yet there is now a generation of theologians who say that Jesus was right about heavenly things, but He was wrong about earthly things.

However, since the Bible gives us enough reliable historical information to conclude that Jesus was a prophet, and since Jesus Himself tells us that the source of this information is absolutely reliable, we have moved not in a circular argument but in a progressive one. We have moved from a starting point of historical openness, to criticism, to historical reliability, to historical knowledge of the teaching of Jesus, to the teaching of Jesus, who tells us that this source is not just somewhat reliable but absolutely reliable because it is nothing less than the Word of God.

When we say that the Bible is the only rule of faith and practice, it is because we believe this rule has been delegated by the Lord, whose rule it is. Therefore, we say that the Bible is inerrant and infallible. Of these, inerrancy is the lesser term; it flows naturally from the concept of infallibility—if something cannot err, then it does not err. In order to pass the test of criticism, the Bible has only to be consistent with its own claims, and if we define truth the way the New Testament does, then there is no valid reason for anyone to dispute the inerrancy of the Bible. If the Word of God cannot fail, and if it cannot err, it does not fail or err.

Chapter Four

CANONICITY

The word *Bible* comes from the Greek word *biblos*, which means "book." However, although the Bible is bound up in one volume, it is not a single book; rather, it is a collection of sixty-six individual books—a library of books. Since there are so many books that together make up the sacred Scriptures, how do we know that the right books have been included in this collection or library of books? That question falls under the issue of canonicity.

We get the word *canon* from another Greek word, *kanōn*, which means "measuring rod" or "norm." To call the Bible "the canon of Scripture" is to say that its sixty-six books together function as the supreme measuring rod or authority for the church. The Bible often has been described as *norma normans et sine normativa*. A form of the word *norm* appears three times in that expression. *Norma normans* means "the norm of norms," and *sine normativa* means "without norm." The Bible is the norm or the standard of all standards, and it is judged by no other standard.

EXTENT OF THE CANON

In our examination of the reliability of Scripture, we have looked at the issues of inspiration, infallibility, and inerrancy. In this chapter, we are considering not the nature of Scripture but rather the scope of it; that is, how far does the canon of Scripture extend?

There are many misconceptions about the canon. Critics argue that, given the large number of books—more than two thousand, they claim—that could have been included in the Bible, it seems probable that some books should have been included but were not, while other books that were not qualified for inclusion made their way in. However, the overwhelming majority of the books considered for inclusion in the canon were quickly and easily dismissed by the early church because they were so obviously fraudulent.

In the second century, Gnostic heretics, claiming Apostolic authority, wrote their own books and disseminated them widely. However, these books were never seriously considered for inclusion in the canon, which is why it is misleading to say that there were more than two thousand potential candidates. If we consider the historical selection process undertaken by the church, a process governed by great caution and careful investigation, we see that only three of the excluded documents were given serious consideration for inclusion in the New Testament: the *Didache*, the *Shepherd of Hermas*, and the First Letter of Clement of Rome. These documents originate from the late first or early second century, and it becomes clear if one reads them that the writers were conscious that their work was sub-Apostolic and post-Apostolic. They thus submitted to the authority of the Apostles and of their writings.

The excluded documents are important and useful for the church, and they have been so throughout church history, but there was never a struggle over whether to include them in the canon. Most of the controversy over the canon in the earlier centuries concerned not what was excluded but what was actually included. Debate went on for some time about whether to include Hebrews, 2 Peter, 2 and 3 John, Jude, and Revelation.

THE CANON ESTABLISHED

Others take exception to the authority of the canon because it was not established until the fourth century, long after the life and death of Christ. Establishing the canon was a process that took place over a period of time; however, that does not mean the church was without a New Testament until the end of the fourth century. From the very beginning of the church, the basic books of the New Testament, those that we read and observe today, were in use, and they functioned as a canon because of their Apostolic authority.

The issue that provoked the establishment of the canon was the appearance of a heretic named Marcion, who issued his own canon. Under the influence of Gnosticism, Marcion believed that the God portrayed in the Old Testament is not the ultimate God of the universe but rather a lesser deity called a "demiurge" who has a nasty disposition, and that Christ came to reveal the true God and to deliver us from this mean-spirited deity. As a result, Marcion expurgated everything in the New Testament that could link Christ in a positive way to Yahweh, the God of the Old Testament. The gospel of Matthew and much material from the other gospels were cut, as was any reference that Christ made to God as His Father. Marcion also eliminated some of Paul's writings. He ended up producing a small, abridged, and edited version of the New Testament. This heresy spurred the church to give an authoritative, formal list of actual biblical books.

THE MARKS OF CANONICITY

In order to determine canonical authenticity, the church applied a threefold test. Some are troubled by the fact that there was a selection process, but the thoroughness of the process should reassure us.

The first mark or test used to verify a book's authority was its Apostolic origin, a criterion that had two dimensions. To be of Apostolic origin, a document had to have been written either by an Apostle or under the direct and immediate sanction of an Apostle. The book of Romans, for example, was not in question because everyone acknowledged that it had been written by the Apostle Paul and thus bore Apostolic authority. Likewise, neither the gospel of Matthew nor the gospel of John was questioned because they were written by Apostles of Jesus. The gospel of Luke was not questioned because Luke was an associate of Paul and traveled with him on his missionary journeys. Likewise, Mark was seen as the spokesman for the Apostle Peter, so the authority of Peter stood behind the gospel of Mark. From the very beginning, there was no doubt about the Apostolic authority and biblical canonicity of the four Gospels or of the basic corpus of Paul's writings.

The second mark for acceptance into the canon was reception by the primitive church. The epistle to the Ephesians is an example that fits this criterion. The assumption is that Paul intended this letter for an audience broader than just the church at Ephesus. It was written as a circular letter, one designed to be disseminated to all the churches in the region around Ephesus. That was true not only of the Ephesian epistle but also of the other epistles of Paul. The Gospels were widely circulated among first-century congregations as well. As a matter of historical reconnaissance, the church, when considering what to include in the canon, took into account how a particular document had been received and quoted as authoritative from early on.

In the First Letter of Clement, which was not recognized as canonical, Clement cites Paul's letter to the Corinthians, showing that 1 Corinthians had been received by the early Christian community as authoritative. In the Bible itself, the Apostle Peter makes mention of Paul's letters as being included among the category of Scripture (2 Peter 3:16).

The third mark of canonicity was the cause of most of the controversy. The books deemed to be Apostolic or sanctioned by an Apostle, and also received by the early church, made up the basic core of the New Testament and were accepted into the canon without any real controversy, but there was a second level of books about which there was some debate. One of the issues concerned the compatibility of the doctrine and teaching of these books with the core books. This is the issue that provoked some of the questions about the book of Hebrews. A portion of this epistle, Hebrews 6, has often been interpreted as indicating that those redeemed by Christ can lose their salvation, a teaching out of sync with the rest of biblical teaching on that subject. However, that chapter may be interpreted in such a way that it is not out of sync with the rest of the Scripture. What finally swung the debate regarding Hebrews was the argument that Paul was its author.

The church in the early centuries believed that Paul was the author of Hebrews, and that landed the epistle in the canon. Ironically, there are few scholars today who believe that Paul wrote it, but there are even fewer who would deny that it belongs in the canon.

THE SCOPE OF THE CANON

A dispute arose in the sixteenth century between the Roman Catholic Church and Protestants over the scope and extent of the Old Testament Scriptures, specifically over the Apocrypha, a group of books produced during the intertestamental period. The Roman Catholic Church embraced the Apocrypha; the Reformation churches, for the most part, did not. The dispute centered on what the first-century church and Jesus Himself had accepted as canonical. All the evidence from Palestine indicates that the Jewish Palestinian canon did not include the Apocrypha, whereas many in Alexandria, the cultural center for Hellenistic Jews, did include it. However, more recent scholarship suggests that even the Alexandrian canon recognized the Apocrypha only at a secondary level, not at the full level of biblical authority. So the question remains as to who was right, the Roman Catholic Church or the Protestants? In other words, by what authority do we determine what is canonical?

According to the Protestants, each book found in the Bible is an infallible book, but the process undertaken by the church as to which books to include was not infallible. We believe that the church was providentially guided by the mercy of God in the process of determining the canon and thereby made the right decisions, so that every book that should be in the Bible is in the Bible. However, we do not believe that the church was inherently infallible, then or now. By contrast, the Roman Catholic formula says that we have the correct books because the church is infallible and anything the church decides is an infallible decision. In the Roman Catholic understanding, the formation of the canon rests on the authority of the church, whereas in the Protestant understanding, it rests upon the providence of God.

I would commend to you further study of the development of the canon. Let me emphasize in conclusion that even though there was a historical sifting process, I believe that God led the church to her final conclusion, and that we have no reason to be anything but fully assured that the right books were included in the canon of sacred Scripture.

Chapter Five

AUTHORITY AND INTERPRETATION

A few years ago, I encountered an old friend. We had gone to college together, and during those years he and I had met nightly for Bible study and prayer. We lost touch with each other after college, so I was delighted to see him. During our conversation, he told me that since college his view of Scripture had changed; he no longer believed in the inspiration of the Bible. Instead, he said, he had come to believe that spiritual authority lies with the church.

HISTORICAL DEBATE

In the final analysis, is the ultimate, unquestionable authority for the church found in the Apostolic words of sacred Scripture or in the body of teachers who currently serve as overseers of God's flock? That was the issue debated in the sixteenth century, at which time the Reformers determined that Scripture alone is the ultimate, authoritative revelation of God; the church does not have authority on an equal footing with Scripture. However, when the Roman Catholic Church convened at the Council of Trent in the middle of the sixteenth century to respond to the Reformation, the fourth session of that council addressed the relationship of the authority of the church and the authority of Scripture. In that session, the church professed confidence in the inspiration and authority of the Bible while also claiming that God reveals Himself through the tradition of the church.

We can find the truth of God in places besides the Bible. We can find it in sound books on theology, insofar as they are sound, but they are not the original source of that special revelation. However, the Roman Catholic Church holds to a "dual-source theory" in which there are two sources of special revelation, one of which is Scripture and the other of which is the tradition of the church. This theory has the effect of placing the church on an equal footing with the Bible itself in terms of authority.

The fourth session of the Council of Trent was dismissed abruptly when war broke out on the Continent, so some of the records of what actually occurred at the council are unclear. In the original draft of the fourth session, the decree read that "the truths . . . are contained partly [*partim*] in Scripture and partly [*partim*] in the unwritten traditions." But at a decisive point in the council's deliberations, two priests rose in protest against the "*partim . . . partim*" formula. They protested on the grounds that this view would destroy the uniqueness and sufficiency of Scripture. All we know from that point on is that the words "partly . . . partly" were removed from the text and replaced by the word "and" (*et*). Did this mean that the council responded to the protest and perhaps left the relationship between Scripture and tradition purposely ambiguous? Was the change stylistic, meaning that the council still maintained two distinct sources of revelation? We do not know the answer to those questions strictly from the records of the Council of Trent, but we do know the answer from subsequent decrees and decisions of the church, most recently in the papal encyclical *Humani Generis* (1950), in which Pope Pius XII put forth with no ambiguity that the church embraces two distinct sources of special revelation.

So, the Roman Catholic Church appeals to both the tradition of the church and the Bible for its doctrine, which is what makes ecumenical dialogue very difficult. When a particular doctrine falls under scrutiny, Protestants want to establish their position strictly on the authority of the Bible, whereas Rome wants to include the renderings of church councils or papal encyclicals. We see this with issues such as the immaculate conception of Mary. Although no such doctrine is found anywhere in the Scriptures, Roman Catholics establish the doctrine on the basis of tradition.

In response to those who uphold *sola Scriptura*, the Roman Catholic Church argues that since it was by the church's decision that certain books were formally included in the canon, the authority of the Bible is subject to the authority of the church and, in a very real sense, the Bible derives its abiding authority from the even greater authority of the church itself. Protestants reject that for biblical, theological, and historical reasons. The Reform-ers restricted binding authority to the Scriptures because they were convinced that the Scriptures are the Word of God, and that God alone can bind the conscience and has absolute authority.

The Roman Catholic Church does claim that God alone is the ultimate authority, but it argues that He has delegated that authority to the church, which is what they believe happened when Jesus said to Peter, "You are Peter, and on this rock I will build my church, and the gates of hell shall not prevail against it" (Matt. 16:18). The author-ity of Peter and the Apostles then passed to their successors in what is called "Apostolic succession." The Roman Cath-olic formulation of this belief asserts that the bishop of Rome, the pope, sits in Peter's place as his successor and so exercises the authority of Peter as Christ's representative on earth.

Whether the Bible clearly affirms Apostolic succession is open to dispute, and controversy continues as to exactly what Jesus meant at Caesarea Philippi when He said that He would build His church on the rock. We do know that there was a delegation process. Christ is the delegated Apos-tle par excellence, as was shown when He said, "I have not spoken on my own authority, but the Father who sent me has himself given me a commandment—what to say and what to speak" (John 12:49). Christ claimed to speak with nothing less than the authority of God, so when the church embraces Christ as Lord, it is recognizing that Christ has authority as the head of the church and is therefore superior to any other part of the church.

In saying that it had "received" Scripture, the church recognized that the books of the canon have binding authority over all. The church was not so arrogant as to claim that it was creating the canon or that the canon received its authority from the church. If God were to appear before me today and I were to ask Him to verify His identity as God, and if He were to do so in such a way that I could not help but bow before His authority, my acquiescence to His authority would not bestow on Him any authority that He did not already have. I would merely be recognizing the authority that is already there and bowing before it. That is exactly what the church did during the early centuries when it was involved in the process of formally recognizing the canon of Scripture.

The church is always subordinate to the authority of the Bible. This does not mean that the church has no authority. Governments and parents have authority, but those authorities have been delegated by God. They do not have the absolute authority that goes with God's own Word. So any authority held by the church is subordinate to the authority of Scripture.

INTERPRETATION

Even if we agree on the authority of Scripture, we are still left with the question of how to be responsible interpreters of the Bible. We are not infallible, and at some point we might distort the Scriptures. That is why we need to learn something about the basic principles of biblical interpretation.[*]

Without going into detail regarding a comprehensive system of hermeneutics, we would do well to consider a few basic principles of biblical study. The first is that the text of Scripture is to be interpreted by grammatical-historical exegesis. *Grammatical-historical* is a technical term

---

[*]   R.C. Sproul, *Knowing Scripture*, rev. ed. (Downers Grove, Ill.: InterVarsity, 2009), provides a layman's guide to the fundamental principles of how to interpret the Bible in such a way as to avoid misunderstanding, misinterpretation, or distortion of the Word of God.

that refers to the process by which we take the structures and time periods of the written texts seriously as we interpret them. Biblical interpreters are not given the license to spiritualize or allegorize texts against the grammatical structure and form of the text itself. The Bible is not to be reinterpreted to be brought into conformity with contemporary philosophies but is to be understood in its intended meaning and word usage as it was written at the time it was composed. To hold to grammatical-historical exegesis is to disallow the Bible to be shaped and reshaped according to modern conventions of thought. The Bible is to be interpreted as it was written, not reinterpreted as we would like it to have been written according to the prejudices of our own era.

The second principle is that we are to take account of the literary forms and devices that are found within the Scriptures themselves. This goes back to principles of interpretation espoused by Luther and the Reformers. A verb is to be interpreted as a verb, a noun as a noun, a parable as a parable, didactic literature as didactic literature, narrative history as narrative history, poetry as poetry, and so on. To turn narrative history into poetry or poetry into narrative history would be to violate the intended meaning of the text. Thus, it is important for all biblical interpreters to be aware of the literary forms and grammatical structures that are found within Scripture. An analysis of these forms is proper and appropriate for any correct interpretation of the text.

The third principle is that Scripture is to interpret Scripture. Historically, this principle is called the "analogy of faith." It rests on the belief that the Bible represents a unified, consistent, and coherent word from God. Any interpretation of a passage that yields a meaning in direct contradiction to another portion of Scripture is disallowed. It is when Scripture interprets Scripture that the sovereignty of the Holy Spirit, the supreme interpreter of the Bible, is duly acknowledged. Arbitrarily setting one part of Scripture against another would violate this principle. Scripture is to be interpreted not only in terms of its immediate context but also of the whole context of the Word of God.

It is equally important to deny the propriety of critical analyses of the text that produce a relativization of the Bible. This does not prohibit an appropriate quest for literary sources or even oral sources that may be discerned through source criticism, but it draws a line as to the extent to which such critical analysis can go. When the quest for sources produces a dehistoricizing of the Bible, a rejection of its teaching, or a rejection of the Bible's own claims of authorship, it has trespassed beyond its proper limits. This does not prohibit the external examination of evidence to discover the authorship of books that go unattributed in sacred Scripture, such as the epistle to the Hebrews. A search is even allowable for literary traditions that may have been brought together by a final editor whose name is mentioned in Scripture. It is never legitimate, however, to run counter to express biblical affirmations.

THE SPIRIT'S WITNESS TO SCRIPTURE

While study of the nature of Scripture, the origin of Scripture, the authority of Scripture, the relationship of biblical authority to ecclesiastical authority, the scope of the canon, and so on are important and helpful for becoming good students of Scripture, our knowledge of the Bible cannot remain abstract. If we have an accurate concept of the nature of the Bible and if we are orthodox in our confession of its authority and of the scope of the canon but have no mastery of the content of sacred Scripture, what have we gained? Scripture is given to us not merely as an abstract doctrine; it comes to us as God's divine Word, designed for edification, reproof, correction, and instruction, that we may be fully equipped as men and women of God.

The crisis in our day is not simply over the issue of whether the Bible is infallible, inerrant, or inspired; the crisis is over the content of the Bible. We spend so much time looking at the academic issues of what we call "prolegomena"—the dating, the culture, and the language of Scripture—that pastors can make it through seminary without ever coming to grips with the content of sacred Scripture. We must see the truth of Scripture, as well as its authority.

The Bible, in its content, is true. Therefore, it is relevant not only because it is authoritative but because it instructs us in what we must know of God and of ourselves. The Bible is true in that it is trustworthy, it is reliable, you can depend upon it; there's no fraud, no deceit, and no distortion there. It communicates real states of affairs.

How do we access that truth? By the Holy Spirit. The doctrine that has emerged, principally drawn up by John Calvin, with respect to the Spirit's confirming the truthfulness of Scripture is called the doctrine of the internal testimony of the Holy Spirit. This internal testimony is internal to us: the Holy Spirit bearing witness to our spirits that this is the Word of God. We know that the Holy Spirit testifies inwardly by virtue of what the Scriptures teach about sonship. How do we know that we are sons of God? The Spirit bears witness with our spirit that we are the sons of God. The Spirit likewise give attestation to the truth claims and truthfulness of sacred Scripture.

There is a whole school of Christians who believe that it is at once futile and even ungodly to try to prove the Word of God by such mundane considerations as rational consistency and empirical verification, because that seems to make the Scripture subordinate to human canons of verification and elevates the authority of reason and science above the authority of God. Some have argued that the Bible is self-authenticating or self-attesting. Certainly, the Bible does attest to its own truthfulness; that is, the Bible makes claims that it is the Word of God. Calvin explained the internal testimony of the Holy Spirit in a progressive way. He began by looking at what he calls the *indicia* of Scripture; that is, the objective evidences that Scripture manifests of its being the Word of God. *Indicia* refer to objective—not subjective—testable, analyzable, falsifiable, or verifiable aspects of proof: objective evidence. What are the indicators that the Bible is the Word of God? Calvin went through two lengthy chapters of evidences for the Bible's claim to be the Word of God, and he recognized that for the Bible to be consistent with its claim, it must be internally consistent and not be filled with contradictions. Calvin tried to proceed on the basis of objective evidence to prove that the Bible is the Word of God.

However, there is a difference between proof and persuasion. Calvin said the evidence is there to prove the Bible's claim and to bring people into a state of moral culpability; that is, the evidence is sufficiently clear to prove the Bible to be the Word of God that it is a moral matter to submit to it or not submit to it. But man is so prejudiced against it that, in his hardened heart, he will resist surrendering to the evidence itself.

Enter the Holy Spirit. The key point of Calvin's appeal to the internal testimony of the Holy Spirit was not to produce a subjective proof for Scripture, but to call attention to the work of the Holy Spirit in the life of the believer because what the Spirit does, Calvin said, is to work "not on your head but on your heart so that you will acquiesce into the indicia." What does that mean? It means simply to yield, to surrender, to submit to the objective evidence that is there. It's not that the Holy Spirit whispers in your ear a secret argument that is not available to the general public. He confirms in our hearts the truth of the matter as it is displayed for us in the internal and external marks of Scripture in and of themselves.

To be sure, for a long time, much of the activity of the Holy Ghost has been relegated to obscurity in the church, to our detriment. But the danger—where the Holy Spirit is emphasized—is to isolate the Spirit from the Word. Does the Spirit of God lead us? Yes, of course. His principal leading, biblically, is leading His people into holiness, sanctification, and obedience. There is objective evidence that the Spirit of God has produced this Book. The Holy Spirit confirms the Word, and the Word confirms the Spirit.

Do you have doubts about the Scripture? One of the best ways to assuage your doubts is to read it. The more I study Scripture, the more overwhelmed I am by the unbelievable insight and penetrating analysis. In my personal educational background, my training has been principally in the field of philosophy and later in philosophical theology; in the training for that specialty, a great emphasis was placed upon critical analysis. But I have to confess that when I read the Scriptures, I find that the Scriptures criticize me. My brain is still operating when I read the Scriptures, and it's not like I've never been exposed to the theories of higher criticism. In fact, the thing that personally confirms more to me of the truthfulness of Scripture is the fact that I had to be exposed to the most radical higher criticism. The more I check out the problems of Scripture, the more amazed I am at the uncanny, minute, intricate symmetry of the entirety of that Book. The argument that impresses me more than any other argument for Scripture objectively is the uncanny consistency of the Word of God.

About the Author

Dr. R.C. Sproul is founder and chairman of Ligonier Ministries, an international Christian discipleship organization located near Orlando, Fla. He is also copastor of Saint Andrew's Chapel in Sanford, Fla., chancellor of Reformation Bible College, and executive editor of *Tabletalk* magazine. His teaching can be heard around the world on the daily radio program *Renewing Your Mind*.

During his distinguished academic career, Dr. Sproul helped train men for the ministry as a professor at several theological seminaries.

He is author of more than one hundred books, including *The Holiness of God, Chosen by God, The Invisible Hand, Faith Alone, Everyone's a Theologian, Truths We Confess, The Truth of the Cross,* and *The Prayer of the Lord*. He also serves as general editor of the *Reformation Study Bible* and has written several children's books, including *The Knight's Map*. Dr. Sproul and his wife, Vesta, make their home in Sanford.

Get 3 free months
of *Tabletalk*